8 HOURS
TO MASTERING
ACT/SAT
ENGLISH

8 Hours to Mastering ACT/SAT English

Copyright © Chris Gallagher M. Ed.

Cover Design by William Benfer

1st edition published March 1, 2019

Table of Contents

Introduction

The English sections of the ACT and the SAT are not nearly as difficult as they seem at first glance. The majority of the material tests students on skills they learned in elementary school, but probably haven't practiced much since. However, it is essential to understand these foundational concepts in order to do well on the English language and writing sections of these tests. The test writers will use elevated vocabulary and unnecessarily complex sentences to confuse students. Nonetheless, the fundamentals are the same. It is just a matter of knowing how to apply them.

With this in mind, this book was written to refresh students' memories on basic English writing structure, and to help them apply it. The book is devoid of lengthy explanations, and I eliminated unnecessary technical jargon. Instead, the explanations focus on simplifying the material. That being said, the practice questions are level appropriate. Additionally, I have included a large sample of actual ACT and SAT questions for each lesson, or chapter.

This book is different from your average test prep book in a number of ways. First of all, it starts with foundational concepts and how to apply them, rather than working backwards and explaining later. This will have the nice side-effect of helping students do well on the essay writing section of the tests.

Second, the goal of the book is to simplify. Student's don't have to know the definition of the past perfect tense, they just have to be able to identify when it is used. This saves time and effort studying complex grammar concepts. Finally, it is SHORT, yet effective. I know that today's students have very busy schedules. However, if students spend eight hours mastering the concepts in this book, their score on this section should increase substantially. While they're at it, their grammar will also improve!

Lesson 1

English Sentence Structures and Comma Rules

There are four basic sentences structures in English. It is necessary to understand these in order to do well on the English sections of the ACT and SAT. They are the cornerstones of written English. Knowing these structures is essential for understanding comma placement.

All sentences, or independent clauses, in English include a subject (s) and a verb (v). Most sentences also have an object (o). When you are analyzing a test question, it is imperative to be able to identify these word types.

The most basic sentence in English is the <u>Simple Sentence</u>. Here are some very simple examples:

- I like bananas. (S V O)
- I like bananas, apples, and carrots. (S V O O O)
- My mother and father like golf and tennis. (S S V O O)
- Traveling is a wonderful way to learn about other cultures and to meet new people. (S V O O)

   Notice that this one is tricky! Traveling is the subject, "is" is the verb, and "to learn" and "to meet" are objects of the verb "is" even though they look like verbs themselves!

A <u>Compound Sentence</u> is two simple sentences (or independent clauses) joined by a conjunction (FANBOYS- for, and, nor, but, or, yet, so).

Ex: My sister is applying to several universities, but UCLA is her favorite. (SVO conjunction SVO)

It is important to note that a compound sentence <u>must have</u> a second subject and verb after the conjunction. If it doesn't, no comma is necessary! Ex: My sister is applying to several universities but hopes to get accepted to UCLA. (There is not a second subject! If the writer added "she" after the conjunction, then a comma would be necessary.)

A <u>Complex Sentence</u> is a combination of an independent clause and a dependent clause. A dependent clause usually begins with a subordinator (ex: when, while, after, because, etc.), and it is DEPENDENT on more information found in the other clause. In other words, if you cover up the independent clause, the remainder of the sentence will not make sense. **Covering half of a sentence to identify answers on the ACT/SAT is often a helpful strategy.** A comma is only necessary when the dependent clause comes first. Identify the independent and dependent clauses in the following examples. Remember that dependent clauses begin with a subordinator.

- When students are choosing universities, they should consider many factors.
- Students should consider many factors when they apply to universities.

Conditional sentences are also examples of complex sentences.

- If students develop good study habits prior to attending college, they will be more successful.
- Students will be more successful if they develop good study habits prior to attending college.

The final type of sentence in English is a Complex/Compound Sentence. As the name implies, this is just a combination of a complex and compound sentence.

- It is important to consider many factors when students are selecting the universities, and students should consult a college planner to determine the most compatible schools for their situation.

Pay close attention when you see conjunctions and subordinators on the ACT or the SAT!

Practice

- **Identify whether the sentences are simple, compound, complex, or compound/complex.**
- **Write the answer in the space below the questions.**
- **Underline independent and dependent clauses. Remember an independent clause IS a simple sentence.**
- **<u>Add commas</u> where they are necessary.**

1. Some people like to stay at nice resorts when they travel.

2. Other travelers prefer more adventurous trips and choose to experience the culture of the country they are visiting.

3. Studying abroad can be a mind-opening experience and it can offer opportunities students might not have considered before.

4. It is imperative to develop critical thinking skills to be successful in college and to make with difficult decisions as an adult.

5. When reading about current events it is important to apply critical thinking and to identify possible bias.

6. The main idea in a reading passage on the ACT is often implied so it is important to be able to analyze the supporting details to find the main idea.

7. Before you attend college it is important to identify your learning strengths because this will help you optimize your time.

8. Students who are strong visual learners will benefit greatly from reading textbooks and students who are audio learners will want to consider recording lectures.

Answers

1. Some people like to stay at nice resorts when they travel. **(Complex Sentence, Dependent clause is second, so no comma is necessary)**

2. Other travelers prefer more adventurous trips and choose to experience the culture of the country they are visiting. **(Simple Sentence, NO SECOND SUBJECT after conjunction)**

3. Studying abroad can be a mind-opening experience, and it can offer opportunities students might not have considered before.
(Compound sentence, comma is necessary)

4. It is imperative to develop critical thinking skills to be successful in college and to make difficult decisions as an adult.
(Simple sentence, "to be successful" and "to make difficult decisions" are both
        objects of developing critical thinking skills, no comma necessary)

5. When reading about current events, it is important to apply critical thinking and to identify possible bias. **(Complex sentence, Dependent clause is first, so comma is necessary)**

6. The main idea in a reading passage on the ACT is often implied, so it is important to be able to analyze the supporting details to find the main idea. **(Compound sentence)**

7. Before you attend college, it is important to identify your learning strengths because this will help you optimize your time. **(Complex sentence, "Before you attend college" is a dependent clause)**

8. Students who are strong visual learners will benefit greatly from reading textbooks, and students who are audio learners will want to consider recording lectures. **(Compound sentence)**

Adjective clauses can sometimes cause students challenges in regards to comma placement. Adjective clauses describe or modify a noun. If you see the words that, which, who, or where, it is most likely an adjective clause. The most important thing to remember when a student sees an adjective clause is to ask if the information is necessary or extra. If the information is extra, then the adjective clause requires commas. See the examples below.

- Social media, which can be very addicting, is rapidly changing the way we interact.
  (*Here the information is extra because we don't need it to identify social media, and the sentence is a complete idea without the extra information*)

- Social media is an invention that has greatly increased our ability to communicate.
  (*Here the information is necessary because it identifies what the "invention" is doing. If we were to write "Social media is an invention.", the reader would say "so what". We all know that it is and invention.*)

If there is a proper noun before the adjective clause, it most likely needs commas.

- Mexico, which is located south of the United States, offers a diverse variety of natural environments.

- Professor Gallagher, who teaches English, traveled to Japan last year.

One helpful strategy when deciding whether the sentence needs commas or not is to cover up the adjective clause with your hand and read the sentence. If it makes sense without the clause, it probably needs commas.

Sometimes using commas around an adjective clause conveys a different meaning than not using commas.

- We took some students to the beach last Saturday. The students who wanted to try surfing all jumped in the water excitedly.
- We took some students to the beach last Saturday. The students, who wanted to try surfing, jumped in the water excitedly.

Which of the two sentences above is referring to "all" of the students?

The second sentence refers to all of the students. Being able to specifically identify meaning derived from punctuation/grammar is extremely important on the ACT/SAT.

Determine whether or not the following sentences need commas.

1. The woman who lives next door to me has three dogs.

2. There are many disadvantages of social media which is changing the way we communicate.

3. The news had a report about a man who robbed the local bank.

4. Critical thinking is a skill which is very important for success in college.

5. Studying abroad is an experience which changes one's perspective on the world.

6. Over spring break, I visited Notre Dame which is located in South Bend, Indiana.

7. Over spring break, I visited several universities which were located in the southeast.

8. The scientists who are researching mental illness are making wonderful progress.

9. Mental illness is being studied by Dr. Jordan who is making great progress.

10. Studies have shown that students who find a special place to study during their university years tend to achieve higher grades.

Answers

1. The woman who lives next door to me has three dogs. **(No comma is necessary. The information is necessary to identify the woman. Which woman are you talking about?)**

2. There are many disadvantages of social media, which is changing the way we communicate.
(The adjective clause is extra information.)

3. The news had a report about a man who robbed the local bank.
(No comma. The information is necessary to identify the man.)

4. Critical thinking is a skill which is very important for success in college.

(This one is tricky, but we all know that "critical thinking is a skill", so it doesn't really make sense without the extra information. The adjective clause defines the skill of critical thinking.)

5. Studying abroad is an experience which changes one's perspective on the world.
(Similar to number 4)

6. Over spring break, I visited Notre Dame, which is located in South Bend, Indiana.
("Notre Dame is a proper noun, so a comma is necessary. Also, the information is extra.)

7. I visited several universities, all of which were located in the southeast, during my spring break. **(The information describing the universities is extra. We already know they are the ones the person visited.)**

8. The scientists who are researching mental illness are making wonderful progress.
(No comma is necessary. The information is necessary to identify which scientists. However, you could add commas, but it would change the meaning.)

9. Mental illness is being studied by Dr. Jordan, who is making great progress. **(Proper noun, the information is not necessary to identify the doctor.)**

10. Studies have shown that students who find a special place to study during their university years tend to achieve higher grades.**(The information is necessary to identify "which students", so no comma is necessary.)**

**Sentence Structure/Grammar Trick #1-
Separating subjects from verbs with adjective
clauses.**

**SAT and ACT writers will often use adjective
clauses to distract readers. When you see
adjective clauses, cover the info and see if the
subject matches the verb. See the example below.**

Rapidly evolving technologies, which are
changing the way we work, is also generating a
substantial amount of controversy.

Answer: The writer needs to change "is also" to "are also". "Technologies" is the subject of the sentence and "are" is the correct verb to be associated with technologies. We will examine this more in the Subject/Verb Agreement section later in this book.

 Trick #2: Adjective Clause Pronoun Trick

Another way the SAT and ACT exams will test your knowledge about adjective clauses is in regards to placing the correct pronoun in the clause. See the example below.

There may not be much of a problem with apples that are not naturally very sour, such as Fuji, but for apples that are known for this, such as Granny Smith, there can be a problem with consumers that will reject apples for lacking that mouth puckering flavor.

UGH! This is typical SAT type of sentence-long and confusing! We need to divide it up. There are two adjective clauses here. Can you find them? One of them has a mistake. Which one?

Answer

The first adjective clause describes apples that are not sour. This clause is correct. The second adjective clause describes consumers "that will reject apples for lacking that mouth puckering flavor". The word "that" needs to be changed to "who" because it describes consumers, or people.

Trick #3- Proper noun/adjective clause introduction

When the adjective clause is describing a proper noun and the information is unnecessary or extra, you don't need a pronoun to introduce it. See the example below.

Fix the following sentence.

Ex: Mexico, located south of the United States, is a country rich in resources.

A. it's located
B. that is located
C. they're located
D. No Change

The correct answer is "no change". A writer could put "which is located...", but "which" is not necessary, and this answer isn't an option.

Sample ACT/SAT questions to test your knowledge of sentence structure and adjective clauses.

1. Therefore, businesses can install solar panels, <u>these are</u> panels placed on workplace roofs to catch and funnel sunlight and convert it to energy.

A) those being
B) they are
C) which are
D) No Change

2. The Great Wall of <u>China, built</u> during the Ming Dynasty, was sturdier than the older version of the wall.

A. China, was
B. China had been
C. China, which,
D. No Change

3. Microchips change rapidly, <u>it</u> allows designers to install more functions.

A) that
B) this
C) which
D) No Change

4. Jane Goodall has been studying chimpanzees, since 1960 which was when she first traveled to Africa.

A. chimpanzees' since
B. chimpanzees, since 1960,
C. chimpanzees since 1960,
D. No Change

5. Before running for President of the
United States, Barrack Obama, was
a senator representing the state of Illinois.

A. United States, Barrack Obama
B. United States Barrack Obama,
C. United States, and Barrack Obama
D. No Change

6. Studies have shown that employees are happier,
healthier, and more productive when they are given
ample vacation time.

A) healthier, being more
B) healthy, and more
C) healthier, and they are
D) No Change

7. The person chosen for the design famous
architect Frank Lloyd Wright, was known for
his innovative approach.

A) design, famous architect Frank Lloyd Wright,
B) design, famous architect, Frank Lloyd Wright,
C) design, famous architect Frank Lloyd Wright, and
D) No Change

8. The physical demands were especially
strenuous for the women because
their costumes, they consisted of confining
corsets.

A. their costumes
B. of their costumes, they
C. of their costumes
D. No Change

Answers

1.C *The word "these" would signal a new sentence, and there is no period. This is an adjective clause and should be introduced by "which are".*

2.D *At first glance, many students might chose "C" on this one, but you don't need a comma after which. The "Great wall of China" is a proper noun and you don't need a pronoun to introduce the adjective clause, so "D" is correct.*

3.C *As with number one, the word "it" would signal a new sentence. This is an adjective clause and the information is extra. The clause should be introduced with "which".*

4.C The adjective clause "which was when she first traveled to Africa" is extra information and needs a comma before it. There is no comma necessary before "since 1960".

5. A *This is also a complex sentence, but the dependent clause is first and ends with United States. The rest of the sentence is the independent clause and doesn't need any commas.*

6. D *This is simply a list. It doesn't need an extra subject or verb (they, being). Healthy doesn't make since because it doesn't match the other two objects forms. Don't overthink it!*

7. A The adjective clause is "famous architect Frank Lloyd Wright", and it is extra information, so it is set off by commas.

8. A This is a complex sentence. "Costumes" is the subject in the dependent clause. There is no need to repeat it with the pronoun "they".

If you can master sentence structure, you will be able to chop up those test sentences and destroy the English sections of the ACT/SAT!!!

<u>Lesson 2</u>

Subject/Verb Agreement

Fundamentally, subject/verb agreement is quite simple when the subject is a person or a physical thing, as shown below with verbs "to be" and "to study".

I- am/study
We- are/study
You- are/study
He/she- is/studies
Scott- is/studies
Mark and Kathy- are/study
It- is/studies
They -are/study

However, when the subject is not a person or a physical thing, it becomes a little more confusing.

EX: **Communication is...**

(Here the subject of communication is an *it* *(singular),* so the correct verb is "is".)

EX: **Different types of communication are...**

(Here the subject is different types of communication. Since it is plural, different types of communication is a "they", so the correct verb is "are".)

Then there are words like team, family, and media. What verb goes with these?

> Ex: **All of the teams in the tournament <u>are</u> good.** (There are multiple teams, so *they are).*

> EX: **However, the team wearing the blue uniforms <u>is</u> the best.** (Even though a team is made up of   more than one person, it is still just one team. So *it is* the best.)

As one can see, subject/verb agreement can get tricky. Often times the questions on the ACT/SAT will also include a prepositional phrase or adjective clause to confuse you.

> Ex: *Weather conditions at this structure, which is located on top of a 6,288-foot peak in New <u>Hampshire, has earned </u>the place the nickname "Home of the World's Worst Weather."*
>
> A. NO CHANGE
> B. Hampshire, have earned
> C. Hampshire has earned
> D. Hampshire, earns

The answer is "B" because the verb "have" refers to "weather conditions". The adjective clause *"which is located on top of a 6,288-foot peak in New Hampshire"* is completely irrelevant to the question. This information is simply there to confuse you. As mentioned in lesson one, when you see information like this on the test, cover it up with your hand. Identify the subject and the verb. Determine whether the subject is singular or plural and make sure it has the correct form of the verb.

Subject/Verb Agreement Exercise- Fill in the blank

1. Family dynamics _____ often defined by culture.
For example, in Latin culture, family _____ the
number one priority.

2. While some people argue that technology _____
helping society progress, others argue that some
types of technology _____ harming society.

3. Linguistics, which is the study of language, _____
an extremely complex and interesting subject. For
example, the ability of children to learn language in
their infancy when they still have little outside
experience upon which to base their understanding,
_____ fascinating.

4. Many people argue that media, especially social
media, _____ (have, has) simply become a vehicle
for propaganda.

5. The political class, which is roughly the 20% of the
population that is educated, _____ expected to play
a significant leadership role in governmental decision

making. The other 80% _____ expected to just follow these ideas.

6. Online learning, which utilizes a wide variety of digital technologies, _____ (offer, offers) students many advantages. However, many teachers argue that in addition to being distracting, online learning programs only _____ (offer, offers) opportunity for self-motivated students.

Answers

1. are, is (many families "are", one family "is")

2. is, are ("technology" is singular, "types of technology" is plural)

3. is, is ("Linguistics" is the first subject, "ability of children" is one ability)

4. has ("Social media" is one type of media)

5. is, are ("Political class" is one class, "80%" refers to people and "are" is the verb that goes with the word "people").

6. offers, offer ("online learning" is the first subject, "online learning programs" is the second subject).

Examples from the ACT/SAT

1. Like any other health problems,
these sicknesses can increase employee absences,
which, consequently, <u>is</u> costly for employers.

A) have been
B) are
C) is being
D) No Change

2. These fast food restaurants, which constituted the
first restaurant chain in the United States, <u>was unique
for its</u> cheap prices and quick service.

A) No Change
B) were unique for their
C) was unique for their
D) were unique for its

3. Utilizing a master schedule, which
includes prioritizing daily tasks,
<u>have been</u> proven to increase students'
academic performance.
A) it's
B) are
C) has been
D) No Change

4. This particular skill, combined with a few basic
lessons in reading and writing, <u>were</u> his sole
inheritance to his daughter.

A. are
B. have been
C. was
D. No Change

5. The men combined their skills, recruited a group of investors, and <u>remains</u> in business together for more than thirty years.

A) remained
B) has remained
C) have remain
D. No Change

6. However, some of the earliest examples of art, including paintings and drawings tens of thousands of years old found on cave walls in Spain and France, <u>portrays</u> animals.

A) has portrayed
B) portraying
C) portray
D) No Change

Answers

1. B (the subject is "employee absences")

2. B (the subject is "fast food restaurants")

3. C (The subject is "master schedule")

4. C The subject "skill" belongs with the verb "was".

5. A (the subject is "the men". This is also a parallel structure question because "remained" matches "combined" and "organized")

*6. C This one is tricky because of all that **EXTRA** information. Block it out, and you will quickly see that the subject is "works of art", which goes with the verb "portray". Your grammar software won't catch that one!*

Lesson 3

Subject/Pronoun Agreement

Similar to the previous lesson, the SAT/ACT tests often have several questions that test your knowledge of subject/pronoun agreement. Additionally, these questions will often include an adjective clause to confuse you. Therefore, it is important to know how to identify these questions and navigate them to arrive at the correct answer.

What is a pronoun? Pronouns are words that replace a noun in a sentence. Pronouns include words such as; he, she, him, her, they, them, it, etc.

Here is an example of how pronouns are used: *San Diego's economy is largely based on tourism. It hosts nearly 35 million tourists a year.*

What does the it refer to? Is it talking about the city of San Diego or tourism? Obviously, it is referring to the city of San Diego because "tourism" can't host tourists. What if we changed the sentences to: *San Diego's economy is largely based on tourism. They host nearly 35 million people a year.*

Why would this be wrong? It is wrong because the city of San Diego is just one city, so the pronoun "they" is incorrect because "they" identifies multiple subjects, as in:

There are many tourism businesses in San Diego. They exist because of the 35 million tourists that visit the city each year.

They is the correct pronoun here because it refers to the tourism businesses, which is plural.

Like with subject/verb agreement, one common trick on the ACT/SAT is to place an adjective clause in between the subject and the pronoun to confuse you. Here is an example:

San Diego is a popular tourist destination which hosts 35 million visitors a year, and they have many beautiful resorts as a result.

This is incorrect because in this sentence the pronoun "they" is referring to San Diego, not the visitors. Therefore, the pronoun and verb should be "it has".

Sample Questions

1. This research was limited in the past by
the weight and size of the fossils, as
well as <u>its</u> fragility.

A) there
B) it's
C) their
D) No Change

2. Upon examination of the sample,
the researchers determined that <u>one</u>
had found a new species, a
75-million-year-old crocodile.

A) it
B) they
C) he or she
D) No Change

3. Although the flood left most of the houses intact,
the surge of water that tore through the neighborhood
in 2006 stripped away the majority of trees and plants
<u>in their</u> path.

A) on it's
B) on their
C) in its
D) No Change

4. In May, voters in the remaining member
States will elect a new European Parliament,
and consequently, <u>it</u> will end the majority that the two
main political groups have enjoyed.

A) No Change
B) their
C) there
D) they

5. The main sign of this type of spider
bite are the red marks surrounding <u>them</u>.

A. it.
B. these.
C. one.
D. No Change

6. However, the success of crowdfunding may reduce
support for the arts if everyone begins to feel that
paying for the art appreciated<u> by them</u> is someone else's
prerogative.

A) he or she loves
B) they love
C) by him or her
D) No Change

Answers to ACT/SAT Sample Questions

1. "C" "Fragility" is referring to the fossils, so the pronoun should be "their".

2. "B" "Researchers" is the subject, so "they" would be the correct pronoun.

3. "C" The subject of the sentence is "the flood", so the correct pronoun would be "its".

4. "D" The subject is "the voters", so the correct pronoun would be "they".

5. "A" "Spider bite" is singular, so the correct pronoun would be "it".

6. "C" This one is tricky. "Everyone" is the subject, but it is an indefinite pronoun and is treated as singular. Therefore, the pronouns associated with it are "him" and "her".

Trick 1- One pronoun issue to be aware of involves the use of it, its, and it's. Remember that it's means "it is" and "its" is possessive.

Example:

The roof of the house is made with tile, accentuating it's Spanish architecture.

A) NO CHANGE
B) its'
C) its
D) their

"Its" is the correct answer because it refers to the tile, which belongs to the roof of the house.

Trick 2 involves the use of indefinite pronouns such as everyone.

EX: Which answer is correct? Everyone has to choose his/her/their path.

The correct answer is his or her because everyone refers to each one!

Lesson 4

Verb Tense and Parallel Structure

Verb tense and parallel structure questions are extremely common on the ACT and the SAT. Verb tense refers to **when** something is happening as identified by the verbs in a sentence. Parallel structure refers to the repetition of word forms in a sentence. The majority of the time, these questions ask you to identify a variety of verb tenses or forms and make sure they match each other in the correct form.

Sometimes these questions test your knowledge of subject/verb agreement AND verb tenses. Therefore, it is imperative to master the previous lesson before completing this one!

You don't need to be a grammar guru to answer these questions. However, there are some important keys to identifying them and answering them correctly. First, identify whether the actions in the paragraph are happening in the past, present, or future. Second, identify what tense the verbs should be in. There are usually time words or phrases to help you. Examples of these include: *nowadays, in the past, in the future, etc.* Finally, find the other verbs in the sentence or paragraph and make sure the tenses match.

In addition to paying attention to verb tense, students also need to be aware of verb form. When verbs are in the subject position or object position, they take on the infinitive form (to + verb) or the gerund form (verb + ing). These also need to match for parallel structure.

Example

"Learning a new language can be challenging, but to miss this experience would be a mistake."

The second verb "miss" should be "missing" to match the first verb "learning".

Practice

1. According to research by a prominent doctor, there _____(are, were) two reasons why people are so angry these days.

2. Our ancestors slept 9 and a half hours a night, but many of us are lucky to _____ (sleep, slept, have slept) seven hours every night.

3. Technology has been rapidly changing throughout the last two decades, and people _____(have had, are having) to change with it

4.This is contributing to our stress level. For example, we're always able to take a call or _____ (to respond, responding) to an email.

5. In the past, we spent our time interacting with friends and _____(creating, to create, created) strong communities with our neighbors.

6. Road rage is at an all time high as drivers are distracted by returning texts, checking social media, and even_____ (will read, reading) online articles.

7. As technology continues to progress, we will have to adapt and learn new ways to cope with the pressure and _____ (deal, dealing, will deal) with anger.

8. Some ideas include practicing meditation, establishing technology-free times throughout our day, and _____ (to sleep, sleeping) more.

Answers to practice

1. *are (The sentence is in the present tense as identified by "people are so angry").*

2. *sleep (This one is a little tricky because it is a complex sentence. The first clause is in the past, but the second clause is in the present as identified by "every night").*

3. *have had (The sentence second part of the sentence is still talking about the past two decades.)*

4. *to respond (This matches "to take").*

5. *creating (This matches "interacting").*

6. *reading (This matches "returning and checking").*

7. *deal (This matches "cope").*

8. sleeping (This matches *"practicing and establishing"*).

9. *The paragraph is discussing the future, so the correct verb tense is "will affect".*

Sample Questions

1. Europe's political class is obsessing about its inter-class battles while recent events <u>brought</u> about massive changes that necessitate consideration.

A) has brought
B) were bringing
C) are bringing
D) No Change

2. Researchers from the National Museum of Mexico <u>has relied</u> on this technique to study a fossilized skeleton that was found two years ago under the ruins of a temple.

A) is relying
B) relied
C) have relied
D) No Change

3. But some fruits do not respond as well to the chemical as others <u>did</u>, and some even respond adversely.

A) will,
B) do,
C) have,
D) No Change

4. As the dancers step to the music, they <u>were also stepping</u> in time with their instructor.

A. will also step
B. are also stepping
C. have also stepped
D. No Change

5. The International Energy Agency (IEA) estimates that constructing and running buildings consumes 36% of the world's energy and <u>produced</u> 40% of energy related carbon emissions.

A. produces
B. are producing
C. were producing
D. No Change

6. Studies show that the brain activity of teenagers checking social media is similar to that of their brain activity while they <u>used</u> cocaine.

A) No Change
B) are using
C) have used
D) have been using

Answers

1. "C" The first verb " is obsessing" shows us the sentence is discussing the present.

2. "B" The words "two years ago" signal the past tense.

3. "B" Parallel structure-"Fruits do" so "others do". Additionally, the sentence is describing a fact, so it should be in the present tense.

4. "B" The sentence is taking place in the present tense.

5. "A" Parallel Structure- "produces" matches "consumes"

6. "B" The sentence is comparing two things that happen in the present tense "checking" and "using".

<u>Lesson 5</u>

Modifiers

Modifiers, or modifications, are similar to adjective clauses. They are words or phrases that describe, change, or *modify* the other parts of a sentence.

Ex: Going to the beach, I realized that I forgot my sunscreen.

"Going to the beach" is the modifier as it tells you when the rest of the sentence occurred.

The most common ACT/SAT question involving modifiers asks the student to determine "who" or "what" the modifier is modifying. These questions are looking for specificity. See the following example.

"I realized that I forgot my sunscreen going to the beach".

This doesn't make sense. Who or what was "going to the beach"? The person or the sunscreen? Generally, the modification should be next to the subject or object that it is modifying as in the original example.

Rewrite the following sentences so that the modifier specifically modifies the correct subject or object.

1. Marita found her purse walking home from the park.

2. While playing basketball, my ankle was sprained.

3. The bank robbers got in a car accident texting and driving.

4. Shopping on the internet, your network should be secure.

5. Your password should be strong when banking online.

6. Traveling to Spain, my connecting flight was late.

7. Driving to work, my car overheated.

8. The test wasn't too difficult early in the morning.

Possible Answers
(Answers may vary)

1. Marita found her purse when she was walking home from the park.

2. While I was playing basketball, I sprained my ankle.

3. The bank robbers were texting and driving when they got in an accident.

4. When you are shopping on the internet, your network should be secure.

5. Your password should be strong when you are using online banking.

6. When I was traveling to Spain, my connecting flight was late.

7. While I was driving to work, my car overheated.

8. The early morning test wasn't too difficult.

When you see sentence dependent clauses or phrases in a question, identify what they are referring to. _Specificity is very important on these exams!_

Sample Questions

1. <u>Laying in the grass, the inspiration
for my book came to me.</u>

A. The inspiration for my book came
to me laying in the grass
B. The inspiration for my book came to
me when I was laying in the grass.
C. Laying in the grass was when
the inspiration for my book came to me.
D. No Change

2. Making a fortune after establishing a major online investing
company in the nineties, <u>millions of dollars were left</u> by Sanders
<u>to charities.</u>

A. Sanders left millions of dollars to
charities.
B. millions of dollars were left
from Sanders to charities.
C. and millions of dollars were
left by Sanders to charities.
D. No Change

3. Testing a drone for shark detection
 off the coast of South Africa,<u> two men
struggling to swim were spotted by
lifeguards.</u>

A. lifeguards were spotting
two men struggling to swim.
B. two men struggled to swim
were spotted by lifeguards
C. lifeguards spotted two men
struggling to swim.
D. No Change

4. Rather than implementing stricter
regulation, hackers should be targeted
more aggressively by government regulators.

A. regulation government regulators
should target hackers more aggressively.
B. regulation, government regulators should
target hackers more aggressively.
C. regulation hackers should be targeted
more aggressively by government regulators
D. No Change

5. Riding on the train, the students took
the time to learn some Italian.

A. some Italian was learned by
the students who wanted to use
the time wisely
B. some Italian was learned by
the students.
C. the students took the time
to learn some Italian while sitting
on the train.
D. No Change

6. Despite efforts to decrease texting
while driving, a large percent of accidents
are still being attributed to this behavior
by law enforcement.

A. a large percent of accidents by
law enforcement are being attributed
to this behavior.
B. law enforcement is still attributing
a large percent of accidents to this
behavior.
C. accidents are largely still being
attributed by law enforcement to
this behavior.
D. No Change

Answers

1. The correct answer is "B". This is the only answer that shows that "the inspiration" came from a person. The rest of the answers are incorrect because they either imply that "the inspiration" was laying in the grass, or it is unclear where the inspiration came from.

2. The correct answer is "A". "Sanders" is the one who made a fortune establishing an online trading company.

3. The correct answer is "C" because it was "the lifeguards" that were testing the drone. "A" is incorrect because "were spotting" is the wrong verb tense.

4. The correct answer is "B" because it is "the government regulators" that would implement stricter regulations. The comma is necessary because the information preceding it is a dependent clause (incomplete sentence of idea).

5. The correct answer is "D" because "the students" were the ones riding on the train. "C" is not the best answer because it is redundant. (We will cover redundancy later in this book).

6. The correct answer is "B". "Law enforcement" is making efforts to decrease texting while driving.

<u>Lesson 6</u>

Transition Words

The correct use of "transition words" is a commonly tested skill on the ACT/SAT. There are two aspects of the use of transition words the tests focus on. The first is meaning, and the second is structural. See the chart below for definitions of the words, and examine the explanation of correct structural use.

Transition Words	Use	Example
Additionally, in addition, furthermore, moreover, also	To add an idea (*use these instead of "and"*)	Climate change is affecting the temperature of the ocean. Furthermore, it is causing stronger hurricanes.
Therefore, consequently, as a result, thus	To show cause and effect (*use these instead of "so"*)	The weather report says it is going to rain on Saturday. Therefore, the soccer game has been cancelled.
However, nevertheless	To show an unexpected result (*use these instead of "but"*)	Hurricanes are getting stronger due to rising temperatures on the planet. Nevertheless, there are still many people who don't believe in global warming.
However, on the other hand, conversely	To show contrast (*usually conversely is only used to show the exact opposite*)	Students who are strong readers and writers tend to do better on the ACT; however, students who are strong in math generally perform better on the SAT. Water freezes at 0 degrees Celsius. Conversely, it boils at 100 degrees Celsius.

Similarly, likewise	To show similarity	Students who are strong readers tend to do perform better on the ACT; similarly, students with strong critical thinking skills perform better on the ACT.
For example, for instance	To give an example	There are several reasons to learn a second language. For example, it may give you more job opportunities.
Indeed, in fact	To emphasize	Learning to speak a second language is an important aptitude. In fact, studies have shown that it can change and enhance brain function.
That is, In other words	To explain or restate	Coral reefs are rapidly dying around the world. In other words, the next generation may not be able to enjoy these beautiful underwater habitats. *Watch out for redundancy with these! Redundancy is a topic that is explained in the next chapter.*
First, second, next, then, finally	To show time or sequence	Self-explanatory Pay special attention to these on the ACT/SAT when asked questions like: "Where should the writer put this sentence?"

Notice that there are two different methods of punctuation used with transition signals. One is with a period, and one is with a semi-colon. Both forms require a comma after the transition word. Both structures are correct. *It is important to know these because there is always at least one question about this on the tests!!!*

Fill in the blanks with the best transition signal from the chart. There may be more than one correct answer.

1. Federal government powers are essential for addressing international affairs. _____ if each state had different trade policies, it would be very difficult to conduct business._____, we must have a federally regulated military for international conflict resolution.

2. Studies show that nearly half of Americans would have trouble affording a $400 emergency. _____ many people think that high schools should start offering basic finance courses.

3. One might think that many people just don't have a lot of liquid assets. _____ an examination of average net worth shows that most Americans don't have many non-liquid assets either. _____ median net worth in America has declined more than 25% in the last 30 years. _____ American consumerism continues to increase.

4. Many people believe that more income will make them feel more satisfied. _____ studies have shown that despite increased income in several countries over the past half a century, the levels of satisfaction of the citizens in these countries remains the same. _____ members of capitalist societies often feel more unsatisfied, no matter how much they earn and consume, because they see their neighbors making and spending more.

5. Economists point to credit card debt as the main contributor to the lack of household savings. _____ it could be argued that student loan debt is just as guilty of a culprit. _____ student loan debt has doubled in the last 15 years. _____ it is projected that 40% of borrowers will default by the year 2023.

Transition Signal Answers

Fill in the blanks. (There are multiple possible answers for most of the questions).

1. A. *For example, For Instance,*
   B. *Similarly, Likewise,*

2. A. *Consequently, Therefore, As a result, Thus,*

3. A. *However,*
   B. *In fact,*
   C. *Nevertheless, However,*

4. A. *However, On the other hand, Conversely*
   B. *In fact,*

5. A. *However,*
   B. *In fact,*
   C. *Additionally, In addition, Moreover, Furthermore, Also, Therefore, As a result, Consequently (Here the writer can use a transition signal to show the information as extra information or to show a cause and effect relationship.)*

Sample Questions

1. There is no question that too much screen time has a negative effect on children's health. As a result, because of other external factors, it is hard to measure these negative effects specifically.

A) DELETE the underlined portion.
B) However,
C) Furthermore,
D) No Change

2. In most developed countries, women are given 6 months to a year off for maternity leave. Additionally, women in the United States are usually only allowed a two to eight weeks.

A) In contrast,
B) For example,
C) Consequently,
D) No Change

3. Studies show that good preschool education helps children prepare for school and do better on standardized test; for example, many wealthy countries are starting to provide public preschool options.

A) indeed
B) consequently,
C) furthermore,
D) No change

4. Producing the materials to build structures causes more pollution than many realize. Therefore, cement-making produces 6% of the world's carbon emissions.

A) Nevertheless,
B) For example,
C) Additionally,
D) No Change

5. Surprisingly, wood is one of the most environmentally conscious building materials. The energy used to produce a wood beam is one-sixth of that used to make a steel beam of comparable strength. Moreover, new trees can be planted when mature ones are cut down, and these will capture more carbon.

A) Similarly
B) Nevertheless,
C) Alternatively,
D) No Change

Answers

1. "B" *The information in the second sentence is showing contrast. It is basically saying that even though something is true, it is hard to prove it.*

2. "A" *Again, the information in the second sentence is showing contrast. It shows how the policy in the U.S. is <u>different</u> from other countries.*

3. "B" *The information in the second sentence is showing an effect of the cause in the first sentence.*

4. "B" *The information in the second sentence is showing an example of the statement in the first sentence.*

5. "D" *The information in the second sentence expands on the explanation in the previous sentence. It is additional information.*

When you see a transition word in the question or the possible answers, it is most likely a question about transition words! Pay attention to the structure- either a period or a semi-colon comes before the transition word, and a comma comes after it. If the transition signal is after a period, it is capitalized. If it is after a semi-colon, it is not capitalized.

<u>Lesson 7</u>

Redundancy

There is a reason why the term "more better" sounds terrible. The reason is that it is redundant. Basically, when someone says "more better", they are saying the same thing twice. If something is already "better", then it doesn't need the "more" part. If I say I like apples better than oranges, you know what I mean. Saying "I like apples more better than oranges" conveys the same meaning, but adds an unnecessary word.

ACT and SAT writers craft many questions that require you to identify and reduce redundancy. Obviously, the questions are more difficult than the example above, but the basic idea is the same. These questions are easy to answer once you can recognize them. Below are some common examples of redundancy.

important essentials	free gift
absolutely necessary	hanging down
added bonus	I thought to myself
advanced warning	true fact
attach together	initially from the beginning
basic fundamentals	knowledgeable experts
circulated around	close proximity

You get the idea. **Be careful though!** Usually the redundant terms are separated by other information.

Sample Questions

1. When a large nursery in San Diego redesigned their building with solar power, they were able to reduce annual electricity cost by $5,000 <u>each year.</u>

A) yearly.
B) every year.
C) Delete the underlined portion and end the sentence with a period
D) No Change

2. Many families get overwhelmed by the financial burden of sending their kids to college <u>because of the added economic stress.</u>

A. as a result of the added economic stress.
B. as a consequence of the added economic stress.
C. Delete the underlined portion
D. No Change

3. The museum showcased airplanes from a bygone <u>era of times past.</u>

A. era.
B. era that is no more.
C. era of another time.
D. No change

4. The school adopted mandatory rules for the <u>students</u>.

A. students that they were expected to follow.
B. students that they had to follow.
C. students that they had been required to follow.
D. No Change

5. Every year there are innovations to smart phones <u>that customers find new and exciting.</u>

A. ,which customers find new and exciting.
B. that customers find exciting.
C. DELETE the underlined portion and end the sentence with a period.
D. No Change

6. The city passed a <u>budgetary measure</u> to allow for funds to be allocated to infrastructure.

A. monetary measure
B. measure
C. financial measure
D. No Change

Answers

1. "C" *"Annual" means every year. Therefore, any other words that refer to yearly are redundant.*

2. "C" *"Financial stress" and "economic burden" mean essentially the same thing, so the underlined information is redundant.*

3. "A" *"Bygone era" means the same thing as "times past". Any other term that refers to time in the past is also redundant.*

4. "D" *"Mandatory" means something that must be done. Therefore, any answer that includes "had to", "expected to", or "required to" is redundant.*

5. "B" *"Innovations" are all new, so anything else that repeats that idea is redundant.*

6. "B" *"Budgetary" is unnecessary because "to allow funds to be allocated" means generally the same thing as "budgetary".*

👉 **Redundancy questions are very easy to spot and solve once you are able to identify them! Answers that are short and specific are generally better on the ACT/SAT.**

Lesson 8

Last minute Tips and Strategies

Who vs. Whom

"Who" is a subject and "whom" is an object. Whom is usually preceded by a preposition (most often "for" or "by").

Examples:
Who is it better for?
Better for whom?
With whom are you going?

One other trick to distinguishing "who" vs "whom" is to think of "who" as replacing "he/she" and "whom" as replacing "him/her".

Effect vs. Affect

"Effect" is a noun, and "affect" is a verb.

Examples:

Government policy affects the economy.

There are many economic effects that result from government policy.

Missing payments on a loan affects your credit score.

Missing payments on a loan has negative effects on your credit score.

There, Their, and They're

"There" identifies location. "Their" identifies possession. They're means "they are".

Examples
There are my keys.
The car is theirs.
They're going to the store.

Its vs It's

"Its" is possessive. "It's" means "it is". This is confusing because usually an apostrophe signals possession, but not with "it's"! There is almost ALWAYS a question about this on the tests!

Examples
The car is old, and its paint is falling off.
The car is old, and it's falling apart.

Then vs Than

"Then" is used for time. "Than" is used to compare two things.

Examples
I went to the beach, and then I came home.
I would rather go on vacation to the beach than the mountains.

Colon : vs. Semicolon ;

These can be confusing, even for English grammar whizzes. However, there is always a question regarding the use of colons and semi-colons on these exams, so it is imperative to know the difference.

A semi-colon is basically used the same as a period. It divides two sentences. A colon is used to introduce more information. Usually this information is a list. See the examples below.

Semicolon
I'm ready for the test tomorrow; I'm confident I will do well.

I'm ready for the test tomorrow; therefore, I'm confident I will do well.

(Notice the transition signal in this example. You can use a semi-colon before a transition signal that introduces a new topic.)

Colon
I studied many subjects in college: political science, geography,economics, and history.

Sample Question

Striving to achieve her academic <u>goals;</u>
Maya studied day and night.

A. No Change
B. goals,
C. goals, and Maya
D. goals: Maya

And the correct answer is…

"B"!
"Striving to achieve her academic goals" is a
dependent clause. This idea needs more information
to make it complete. Therefore, a semicolon would
not be correct because a semicolon separates two
complete sentences. A colon is incorrect as well
because the dependent clause is not introducing
information such as a list. The word "and" is
unnecessary because "and" is a conjunction that
would once again combine two complete sentences
or independent clauses.

Dashes are sometimes used on the ACT/SAT. One dash serves the same function as a colon. Two dashes around *extra information* serve the same purpose as two commas. The only difference is that dashes show more emphasis than a colon or comma. However, they are used in the same grammatical manner.

Examples *I studied many subjects in college-political science, geography, economics, and history.*

I visited several universities- all of which were amazing- during my spring break.

(You can't use dashes instead of commas in a list- only for extra information!)

Review and Strategies

1. Identify the subjects and verbs in each test question.

2. Determine whether the sentence is simple, compound, or complex.

3. Identify adjective clauses in test questions. **Cover adjective clauses and other extra information with your hand, or even cross it out with a pencil**, and make sure the subject of the sentence matches the verb or pronoun. ACT/SAT writers love to add clutter to confuse students.

4. Determine the verb tenses in each passage or sentence and make sure the they match.

5. Read the information before and after the underlined sections in the passages.

6. Identify transition signals and determine if they convey the correct information. Also, make sure they are used with correct punctuation.

7. **Cover the answers** and try to find the error in the underlined sections **BEFORE** you read the possible answers.

8. Shorter, more concise answers are generally better. Wordy answers are often incorrect. Don't let long answers impress you or confuse you!

9. Statistically, the answer "No Change" is just as likely to be correct as the other answers.

10. When you see words in the question like "most effectively", there may be more than one answer that is *grammatically correct,* but one answer will be more *thematically* correct. In other words, the right answer will have more information that specifically connects to the paragraph. Again, **specificity is the key to choosing the right answers on these tests**.

These tests really aren't that difficult! You don't have to be a grammar whiz to do well, but you do have to know the following basics and how to _apply them_: *sentence structures, independent/dependent clauses, subject verb agreement, pronouns, transition words, and punctuation.*

Know the fundamentals presented in this book and approach the test with confidence!

Made in the USA
Middletown, DE
28 May 2020